# Restoring Restorative Rest

*Proven Tactics to Reduce Insomnia
Without the Guesswork*

Sensei Paul David

# COPYRIGHT PAGE

Restoring Restorative Rest: Proven Tactics to Reduce Insomnia Without the Guesswork, by Sensei Paul David, Copyright © 2020.

All rights reserved.
ISBN# 978-1-7771913-5-1 (E-book)
ISBN# 978-1-990106-06-4 (Paperback)

This book is not authorized for free distribution copying.

# To Check Out The Next Book In This Series Visit:

www.amazon.com/author/senseipauldavid

# Get Our FREE Books Today!

## Click & Share the Links Below

### FREE Kids Books
lifeofbailey.senseipublishing.com
kidsonearth.senseipublishing.com

### FREE Self-Development Book For Every Family
senseiselfdevelopment.senseipublishing.com

## Join Our Publishing Journey!

If you would like to receive FUTURE FREE BOOKS, and get to know us better, please click www.senseipublishing.com and join our newsletter by entering your email address in the pop-up box.

Follow/Like/Subscribe: Facebook, Instagram, YouTube: @senseipublishing

Scan the QR Code with your phone or tablet

to follow us on social media: Like / Subscribe / Follow

# TABLE OF CONTENTS

**FOREWORD** ................................................... ix

**Chapter One  Examining the Restoration of Rest** ................................................. 1
   *Practice Journaling* ........................................ 3
   *Leverage Guided Imagery* .............................. 4
   *Restorative Breathing* .................................... 9
   *Resting the Body and Mind* .......................... 11

**Chapter Two  Proven Hints for Restorative Sleep** .......................................... 14

**Chapter Three  Journaling Your Experiences** ................................................ 30

**Chapter Four  Finding Equilibrium In All Ramifications** ........................................ 38

**Chapter Five  Making Your Bedroom A Sanctuary** .................................................. 50

**Chapter Six  More Ways Of Restoring Rest** ............................................................. 58

**Chapter Seven  Leveraging Yoga For Restorative Sleeps** ...................................... 69

    *The Link Between Yoga And Restorative Sleep* ............................................................................ *70*

    *Yoga Tips* ...................................................... *72*

## Chapter Eight  Sign In And Out In Grand Style ............................................... **75**

    *Why You Need Restorative Sleeps And Rest* .. *76*

    *REM Sleep* ..................................................... *78*

    *Deep Sleep* ..................................................... *79*

    *How To Sign In And Out In Style* ................... *81*

    *Learn The Art of Relaxation* ......................... *82*

## Index ............................................................ **92**

# FOREWORD

Sensei Paul David has always been passionate about adding value to the lives of people. He is an indefatigable researcher who will leave no stone unturned to ensure that the people around him have better experiences every day. His ability to simplify complex concepts such as mindfulness and procrastination, has always endeared him to his teeming readers all over the world. In this masterpiece, David explores how you can eliminate restlessness and restore quality sleep and rest into your life.

He has an uncanny ability to help you convert uncertainty into curiosity in order to help you form beneficial habits of continuous self-education. Apart from his training and expertise, his rich experience installs him as the best person to write this book. In 2017, he was hit by a truck and knocked unconscious while riding his bicycle. Indeed, he protected his head and center-line before impact. Nonetheless, he was left with intense back pain after surviving That started disturbing his sleep.

Just like any other person, David sought solutions to the problem. He saw a neurosurgeon who told him that he was a candidate for spinal surgery. Nonetheless, he decided not to choose that option.

He was determined to find another alternative that would help him solve the problem without surgery. He tried conventional methods, such as spinal injections and acupuncture, alongside other treatments and therapies. Unfortunately, none of them worked in the long run. Therefore, he had to learn to treat himself through some techniques he discovered.

Don't get the thinking wrong - there's no magic potion here. This book is about the strategies and techniques

David learned that helped him to start sleeping like a baby again. So, if you have been suffering from insomnia, this book is for you. David knows what it feels like when every area of your life is malfunctioning because you are not getting quality sleep. That is why he has put this project together. Note that not everything in this book that will work for you.

However, you can be confident that you will find helpful tips that will improve the quality and quantity of your sleep. Reading this material offers you a streamlined synopsis and solution strategies, all in one place. It also provides you with a path to action that can coach and guide you whenever you need it. Besides, it contains a FREE specialized bonus guided meditation to recap the finer points of the book faster and easier than before.

## Thank You from The Author: Sensei Paul David

Before we dive in, I'd like to thank you for picking up this book. Your time is valuable, and I know there are many other similar books and courses out there that offer to help, but you chose to invest in mine, and that means everything to me.

Now that you're here, and if you stick with me, I promise to make our time together valuable and worthwhile.

In the pages ahead, you will find some areas of information and practices more helpful than others - and that's great, because as you apply what works best for you, you will benefit from an exciting transformation of character and knowledge. Enjoy!

# Welcome

"It's very important that we re-learn the art of resting and relaxing. Not only does it help prevent the onset of many illnesses that develop through chronic tension and worrying; it allows us to clear our minds, focus, and find creative solutions to problems."

**Thich Nhat Hanh**

**Proven tips and strategies to help reduce insomnia without the guesswork**

Let's start our journey by exploring the very definition of the word 'restoration'.

*Restoration (noun): the action of returning something to a former owner, place, or condition, e.g. the restoration of peace.*

In today's fast-paced world, it's hard to take time to rest. Everyone is overworked and stressed out. If you are like so many people, then you are a doer who is constantly striving to complete tasks in a timely fashion and still rise to the top. You probably suffer from exhaustion, burnout, and a feeling of being overwhelmed as you try to tackle everything that life throws at you. Many people don't even know how to rest because they can't shut their minds down. In this book, we will explore restoring restorative rest.

**Let us explore ways to restore your restorative rest.**

Congratulations on starting this and enjoy the process.

Sensei Paul

# Chapter One

# Examining the Restoration of Rest

## Bring Tranquillity to your Body and Mind

Indeed, sleeping is a vital component of resting. Nonetheless, resting goes beyond lying down and closing your eyes. Rather, it has more to do with finding emotional balance and inner tranquillity. In fact, one of the reasons you struggle to sleep is that your mind is running from pillar to post. You cannot have quality sleep when you are mentally disturbed due to anxiety. In the same way, you cannot get enough sleep when you are drowned by thoughts of guilt and shame due to your past mistakes.

It is true that you will fall asleep if you are completely exhausted. However, that does not translate to a restful sleep. Why? Your body might shut down into a restful mode. Nonetheless, your mind will continue to race, and this can lead to nightmares. So, it is not enough to sleep for eight hours. It is all futile if you are still feeling emotionally and mentally drained when you wake up.

Therefore, you need to find a way to balance stress and relax to restore your physical and psychological health. This chapter explores tips that can help you begin this process. Here they are:

**Practice Journaling**

Writing is a physical process that has a psychological impact. When you are writing, your mind is also involved. You would have noticed that many individuals have blogs where they write about different topics such as travel, dating, entrepreneurship, and many more.

Of course, there are many reasons people start a blog. Nonetheless, one of them is that it serves as a tool for stress management. Even making daily posts on social media can make you more relaxed than you can imagine. However, you don't have to start a blog to enjoy the numerous benefits of writing. Instead, you can keep a journal.

Take advantage of journaling to write your feelings, experience, goals, and strategies. This activity enables you to be more thoughtful and strategic in your approach to life. You will stop making decisions hastily, and that will improve your performance because you will start making fewer mistakes.

**Leverage Guided Imagery**

One of the ways you can set your mind free from entangling negative emotions is by taking advantage of guided imagery. It involves placing your mind in a particular mental setting that generates positive emotions. The positive feelings will help you create more positive energy, which ensures that you are calmer and more relaxed.

Audiotapes or scripts are used by some people for guided imagery. However, some people turn to a teacher to help them on their journey. Guided imagery helps to free the imagination to disconnect the body from destructive thoughts of the mind. According to Michigan Medicines C.S. Mott Children's Hospital, you can practice guided imagery by taking advantage of some tested and proven tips. (2) They include the following:

## Sit and Take a Few Breaths

Guided imagery begins with sitting in a comfortable location. While in the sitting position, take a few deep breaths, which initiate relaxation.

## Picture and Think

Thinking about a setting that inspires serenity can lead to inner tranquillity. Note that the setting you will choose depends on your personality. For example, if you are an introvert, it is not likely that you consider going to a beach as something that inspires serenity.

However, an extrovert might find peace by thinking about such a setting. An introvert is likely to find a mountain retreat peaceful. Therefore, use a setting that gives you a sense of tranquillity. Picture it in your mind and imagine finding yourself there. Think about what you will see, hear, and feel when you are there.

## Choose a Suitable Pathway and Sound

If you need a path to enter guided imagery, you are not alone. Before you can choose an ideal pathway, you need to first identify what you think can give you a sense of serenity.

For example, if you consider sitting on a beach peaceful, think about the pathway that leads to the place. Go deeper into the reality of the imagination. Note that you cannot have an optimum experience if you have never had an actual experience of that setting.

I mean, you should have been to the beach before and enjoyed the inner peace that comes with sitting there. So, when you imagine being there, you will be able to easily produce similar emotions through guided imagination.

Moreover, you should pick a sound or word that is associated with the setting that gives you a sense of inner tranquillity. When you practice consistently, it will be easier for that word or sound to help you connect with the experience.

**Indulge All Your Senses**

To have the best experience when using guided imagery, you have to indulge all your senses. I mean, if you imagine sitting among trees, you should go beyond the sight. You should also think about the warm breeze caressing your skin. Also, imagine the sound of chirping birds.

When you are done with the guided image tour, open your eyes after counting three. If you have done it properly, you will realize that you will feel more relaxed than you were before the practice.

## Restorative Breathing

There is no life without breath. In fact, it is a subconscious activity that we don't think about unless on a few occasions, especially when we are sick. However, if you can take your time to observe your breath, it can become an interesting means of finding inner peace.

Making your breath in tune with your body can change your life tremendously and make you more aware of your surroundings.

Michigan Medicines C.S. Mott Children's Hospital developed a simple breathing exercise that helps you to gain inner peace. It involves the following steps: (1)

- Take a very deep breath
- Sustain it for awhile
- Let go as you exhale

Ordinarily, this process sounds simple. However, when you try it repeatedly, you will be surprised by the result you will get. You will experience a sense of peace and calmness that will make you want to practice the steps all over again.

Simple breathing exercises such as this helps to cope with depression and anxiety. It also increases muscle relaxation and flexibility. Therefore, it increases the quality and quantity of sleep.

## Resting the Body and Mind

For many years, philosophers were at loggerheads regarding the relationship between the mind and the body. Apparently, one cannot work without the other. So, it is not good enough to rest your body. You must also work on your mind to ensure that your whole being is intact.

The good news is that it is not challenging to achieve tranquillity for both your body and mind. Despite the demands of this habit, it has enormous benefits. The tips below can make a whole lot of difference:

## Have an Aromatic Warm Bath

Start by letting warm water run over your body. Then add aromatic oils or bath bombs into the water for an aromatic experience.

## Enjoy Music

Listening to the pleasant tune of your favourite song while enjoying the warm bath is the perfect body and mind soothing experience. Let loose and sink into the experience as everything around you begins to come alive.

## Practice Mindful Meditation

Many experts believe that meditation would have been a multi-billion dollar industry if it could've been packaged like a pharmaceutical product. This claim is not far from the truth due to the numerous benefits of practicing meditation, that has been scientifically proven.

One of the perks of this practice is that it makes people calmer and more relaxed. So practicing meditation mindfully is one of the best ways you can work on your mind and body to bring them into a tranquil state.

It involves paying attention to your breath and other things in your surroundings. You cannot have the best experiences in life when you are not present in the moment. Meditation helps you to pay attention to every detail, thereby enabling you to enjoy every moment.

# Chapter Two

# Proven Hints for Restorative Sleep

Despite the benefits of obtaining restorative sleep, the process is not as tricky as many people think. This chapter explores proven tips that can make a restorative sleep the norm rather than an exception in your life.

## Have A Regular Sleep And Wake Time

One of the reasons restorative sleep is elusive for some people is due to their irregular sleep and wake up times. Your body needs a consistent routine that it can adapt to. When you incessantly change your bedtime and wake up time, your body will have to adjust all over again. Once your body adjusts to a rhythm, you can be sure that you will wake up more energized and reinvigorated regularly.

## Rejuvenate Yourself With Sunshine

Some people don't realize how much they need sunshine. Indeed, excess of it can cause health risks. However, if you don't have sufficient exposure to sunlight, it can affect your physical and mental health. Your body needs sunshine to feel rejuvenated, thereby energizing you to complete your daily tasks. Ensure that you don't use bright light in your room when the sun sets. It can make your body stay awake and active, thereby ruining the quality and quantity of your sleep.

**Don't Keep Late Nights**

You will disrupt your sleep rhythm when you have a culture of sleeping late. It can be tempting to watch an exciting movie late into the night. However, it is not a healthy practice. Go to bed when you notice that it is getting late. You can always complete the movie some other time.

Moreover, you should ensure that you use your bed for sleeping in the night rather than reading or checking your social media page. Your phone's light can affect your eyes and make it difficult for you to sleep well. This habit will only ensure that you don't have a restorative sleep. You will wake up feeling fatigued and jaded.

## Avoid Napping During The Day

Napping during the day is a sign that you have not been sleeping well. You should not have this habit unless during the periods when you are sick. However, you might need a nap because you are involved in a physically draining activity. In such a situation, ensure that you sleep nothing less than fifteen to twenty minutes to guarantee reinvigoration when you are awake.

## Regular Exercise

The importance of regular exercise cannot be overemphasized. Note that you don't have to hit the gym to participate in exercising. A thirty to forty-five minutes routine at home can go a long way in relaxing your muscles and calming your mind. Yoga is also another option that can help you loosen your muscles to improve your sleep.

## Don't Take Your Stressors To Bed

Stress is inevitable because of its importance to our lives. No one can succeed in life without going through some level of stress. You need stress in your career to push yourself to the top. You also need to put yourself under pressure to keep developing and acquiring skills.

However, a lack of stress management skills can be disastrous. For example, you should avoid taking your stressors to bed. In other words, avoid working late into the night. Let all your activities be in the day. Ensure you complete your tasks during the day and use your night for the one thing it should be used for – sleep.

Besides, unless you are a remote worker, you should avoid taking your job home. You should spend your time at home with your family and loved ones. When you allow your stress at work to affect the quality of time you spend with your family, it will eventually affect your work-life balance, which will take its toll on your mental health.

## Have Bedtime Rituals

Endeavour to create a bedtime routine. This approach will make you start feeling more relaxed when that time approaches. Your body knows what is next, and it will start preparing for it. You can consider a warm bath or listen to soothing music as part of your ritual.

Just use what works for you. You should know those things that make you feel more relaxed and ready to sleep. Do them before you sleep. When you do them consistently, your body will adjust to them. In fact, one will become a trigger for the next as your muscles learn to carry out the routine.

## Watch Your Diet

In case you don't realize it, foods carry chemical energy. In other words, they are chemicals that are capable of reacting with your body to cause reactions. Therefore, it is crucial that you don't take what you eat for granted. Note that what you eat includes what you drink.

Foods and drinks that contain caffeine are energizers. They work in such a way that they will keep your body active. So, it is vital that you don't take them in the evening because they will interrupt your sleep. Even if you sleep, it is likely you wake up an hour later.

In that case, it might become difficult to sleep again. You might find yourself just tossing in bed instead of sleeping. So, endeavour to drink water rather than such drinks, especially in the evening. Sacrificing your sleep will affect your activity the next day.

## Reduce Alcohol Consumption

Many people use alcohol as a stress reliever. Of course, it can have short-term benefits. However, it can cause long-term health issues. So, you need to find healthy alternatives to relieve stress. However, even if you cannot do without the substance, you should avoid taking it after dinner time.

The rationale behind some people consuming alcohol after 6 pm is that it will not affect them when working or doing other daily activities. Nonetheless, taking alcohol before bedtime can disrupt your sleep. If you drink a lot, you can pass out. However, by the time you wake up, you will be feeling horrible and exhausted.

A hangover will set in, and it can make you feel useless all through the following day. It will affect your performance, especially if you are doing a job that is mentally and physically demanding. You might find yourself dozing off for most parts of the day.

## Be Picky With Snacks

Yes, excess consumption of snacks can have adverse effects on your health. However, there is nothing wrong with taking snacks before bedtime. The only consideration is that you should watch the type you consume.

Choose light and bland ones to avoid repercussions. Heavy snacking can leave you waking up with heartburn or an upset stomach.

On the other hand, a soothing snack will help you get the restful night sleep you desire.

**Buy A New Bed**

You should not hesitate to purchase anything that can improve the quality of your life. Unfortunately, many people have a culture of buying luxuries rather than necessities. A good bed is a need you cannot afford to ignore.

Note that a bed does not have to be expensive to offer you restorative sleep. Get something you can afford, that will not strain your body. This action is particularly important if your current bed is not comfortable. It is not healthy for you to wake up with back pains. Act as soon as possible.

**Don't Focus On The Clock**

Many individuals have the habit of watching the clock when they lay down. This is often the case, especially when the position of the clock is where you can easily see it. It is a sign of restlessness if you often check the time when you are already in bed.

If you find that you often do this, you should consider changing the position of the clock or the position of your pillow. Also, find alternative relaxation techniques that can lull you to sleep. Music can be a fantastic option.

**Discard Your Worries Before Bedtime**

You cannot have a restorative sleep if you are worried. There are many potential sources of anxiety in the modern world, including pressure from your job, your bills, and family issues. Social media harassment and bullying can also make you feel bad.

However, you have to avoid taking your worries to bed. Note that being anxious will not solve your problems. You should rather make plans that will help you resolve your issues. Be optimistic if you have not found one. Sleep and hope that the following day will be better.

If you think about it, you will realize that there have been many times you were worried, but you eventually wished you had not been. Many of our fears never come to fruition. So, ensure that you make realistic plans rather than worrying over what the future holds.

## Work On Your Room's Temperature

Your room temperature has to be moderate for you to have restorative sleep. If your room temperature is too high, you will find yourself tossing in bed. On the other hand, if it is too cold, it can leave you waking up with a cough or catarrh.

So, it is imperative that you adjust the temperature of your room to about 70 degrees Fahrenheit or 21 degrees Celsius. According to the publication of the National Library of Medicine, sleeping in a warm bedroom for five days or more will severely impact your ability to gain a restorative rest. It also reduces sleeps time and increase wakefulness. (3)

## Stay off Your Digital Devices In Bed

Many people, especially teenagers, are fond of excessive exposure to digital devices, such as computers, smartphones, and televisions. Meanwhile, this practice harms sleep. A study published by the National Center for Biotechnology Information affirms this claim. (4)

Therefore, endeavour to put down your electronics before bedtime. If you have reasons to use your phone or computer at night, wear glasses that can block out blue light.

A study published in the National Library of Medicine confirms the benefit of this safety measure.

(5) You should also consider using an app, like flux, which blocks the blue light on your computer. Another option is the installation of a blue light blocker on your smartphone.

Interestingly, blue light blockers are available for both iPhones and Androids. You can even find free ones. Finally, ensure you avoid staying in front of your television for up to two hours before you go to sleep. This approach will ensure that you enjoy a restorative sleep regularly.

# Chapter Three

# Journaling Your Experiences

I earlier mentioned journaling briefly. It is a crucial tool for documenting and implementing a sleep pattern that will boost your health and performance in your daily activities. Nothing significant comes by accident. So, you have to be deliberate in ending your debacle with nightmares and waking up feeling exhausted.

One of the ways you can give yourself a new lease on life is by journaling your journey. You need to document your emotions, eating habits, and sleep patterns. This approach will enable you to learn about your body, to make changes where necessary. This chapter explores tips that can make this new journey a success.

## Place A Premium On The Quality Of Your Sleep

There is no doubt that quality nights of sleep have many benefits. However, many people undervalue it. Some people even associate sleeping with laziness. However, this claim is far from the truth. The only time sleeping can be seen as laziness is when you are sleeping when you ought to be working.

I have to reiterate the importance of getting a good night's rest because you can never work towards getting restorative sleep if you don't realize how essential it is to sleep well. It is when you realize that you are missing a lot by not getting enough sleep that you are ready for the next tip.

**Start A Sleep Journal**

Once you are convinced that getting quality sleep is not negotiable in your life, then you are ready to make the necessary changes that can restore your natural sleep pattern. One of the first things you need to do to turn the situation around is to start a sleep journal.

Documenting your experience is the best way to study your body and its sleep pattern. This technique will also help you to notice the changes happening in your body. Besides, it will help you to evaluate the impact of the sleep changes you are making, on the quality of your lifestyle.

## Decide How Often You Will Update It

You should not keep a journal for the sake of it. I mean, you have to decide vital things such as how often you will update it. If not, you will be erratic in your journal entries, and that will be a complete waste of time. Don't choose a schedule that will not be feasible for you.

It is best to update your journal daily. However, if you know that you cannot be faithful to the commitment, you can take an interval of two days. Just ensure that you are consistent going forward. Note that only those that are consistent can enjoy the full benefits of journaling.

## Compare And Evaluate

In case you are wondering what you need to do with the journal, I've got you. You can use it to document the impact of the tips you are learning in this book. Notice the quality of your sleep before you start practicing the hint and the changes after leveraging it.

For example, if you have decided to start winding down thirty minutes before bedtime, notice the quality of sleep you had before you made the change. Depending on the frequency at which you document your experiences, notice what has changed since.

Moreover, your journal should contain the following details:

- Your bedtime
- The duration of your sleep
- The frequency of the times you woke up in the night (if any)
- The beverages and foods you consumed during the day and before you slept
- The way you were feeling before and after
- Your stress level before and after you slept
- Any medications you took
- The regularity and routine of exercise you had
- The quality of your sleep after waking up

## Be Consistent

You are not the first person to make the decision to start and keep a journal. Unfortunately, many people have journals but don't update them. It is good to start documenting your experience in a journal. However, it goes beyond that.

You have to be deliberate about staying consistent. It is when you document your experiences regularly that you can enjoy the benefits of using a journal to restore your natural sleep pattern. So, you must put measures in place to ensure that you continue the commendable art and practice of keeping a journal.

## Be Accountable

One of the best ways you can ensure that you are consistent with your decision to keep a journal is to tell someone you respect about it. If you are in a romantic relationship, you can tell your partner.

This approach will ensure that you will have someone to keep tabs on you. Besides, this method also ensures that you have someone of like mind you can share your progress with. Knowing that you have someone willing to listen to your growth inspires you to continue what you have begun.

## Chapter Four

## Finding Equilibrium In All Ramifications

The dynamism of life demands that you find a balance. You will have to move from one phase to another, and the demands of each stage are not the same. For example, the pressure on a single person is different from that on a married person.

If you are married, and you have a job, you will have to work tirelessly to ensure that you are a responsible parent (if you have kids), an available spouse, and a reliable employee. Maintaining balance in all of these areas is essential to experiencing a restorative sleep. So, this chapter will explore how you can find balance in every area of your life to increase your chances of having reinvigorating and energizing sleep.

## Take A Breather

The fast-paced nature of life can make you caught up in chasing the wind, so that you will ignore some of the most important things in your life, such as your relationships and your health. If you don't slow down sometimes, and take a breather, your health can deteriorate.

Besides, you might end up ruining your relationships because you are struggling to find time for your loved ones. The truth is that relationships die a natural death when we don't invest in them. Meanwhile, the greatest investment a relationship needs to keep growing is time. Time is crucial, especially as a parent and spouse.

You might be surprised that your partner ends up filing for a divorce because he or she feels that you don't care about him or her. So, you need to find a balance between your career and your relationships. When you have issues with your relationship, it can affect the quality of your sleep and your mental health.

**Live In The Moment**

You cannot enjoy life when you don't learn to live in the moment. There are a lot of beautiful things in life, but you can never focus on them when your mind is in a troubled state. The truth is that you will always have reasons to be anxious and stressed.

However, you need to learn to see beyond your troubles and fears. When you are not living in the moment, you can walk through a garden of beautiful flowers and not appreciate the beauty of nature. In the same way, you can be eating a very delicious meal but never realize it because you are anxious.

Don't let your troubles and demands of life weigh you down such that you forget to appreciate the beauty of enjoying the simple things of life. Think about your relationships and other things in your life that make you feel grateful. It is when you approach life this way that you can start getting restful night sleeps.

You need to practice meditation to see beyond the rising bills and job disappointments. Contrary to what some people think, meditation is not a practice that is exclusive to Shaolin monks. It is for anyone who wants to find inner peace and radiate calmness. There are different forms of meditation. Explore them and find the one that works for you. Regardless of the one you choose, you can be certain that your sleep will improve when you are consistent in it.

**Leverage Your Strengths More**

When you don't play to your strength, you will look like a flop. You have to realize that we are all wired differently. You are a unique person who has distinctive features that makes you different from other people. It is okay to have people who are your role models. However, you have to be careful about what you copy from others.

For example, some people only work best when they have to carry out a task in the early part of the day. However, some people thrive better when they have to work in the night. So, you need to discover your strength and abilities. When you do, take advantage of them.

When you work in a situation that allows you to express your abilities, you will become a star at it because of your great performance. This experience will give you a boost and will allow you to have more positive emotions. Consequently, you will have more stillness in your nights.

## Be Patient

Nothing good and sustainable comes easy and fast. It often takes time and a process that cannot be eliminated. So, don't expect your body to adjust immediately to your new sleep schedule. If you have had the habit of sleeping late, your body will still expect you to continue that way.

Change things gradually and maintain consistency. Your career or responsibilities as a parent, especially a nursing mother, might have disrupted your natural sleep rhythm. You will not start sleeping early automatically. Just ensure that you are on your bed earlier than before. Your body will soon pick up the signal and will adopt the new schedule soon enough.

So, don't be frustrated if it seems as though you are not getting results from your new approach. You have to believe in the process and keep at it because it will eventually yield the results you crave.

## Close Up Activities Thirty Minutes Before Bedtime

You should avoid stressing yourself before you sleep, to avoid having difficulties. It is in your best interest to wind down any task at least thirty minutes before bedtime. This approach does not mean that you should do nothing before you sleep.

Rather, take advantage of that period to take a warm bath or listen to soothing music. Checking your phone for social media updates might not be the best idea around this time due to the exposure to the blue light that comes with it. Just ensure you are in a relaxed mood before you sleep.

**Sex Only**

The only intense activity you can do, that will not hurt your sleep, is sex. Indeed, this activity demands a lot of energy. Nonetheless, it ends up relaxing your body to lull you to sleep.

You will be making a mistake if you do something as intense as hitting the treadmill right before you try to fall asleep. It can tense up your muscles, thereby preventing you from having a restful sleep.

## Consider Sleeping Alone

I have deliberately put this tip somewhere close to the end of this chapter because it is not something you should be quick to do. It should be your last resort when you are sure that there is no other way you can go about restoring your normal sleep pattern.

However, drastic times require drastic actions. If you realize that you are struggling to sleep because your partner snores or tosses around in bed, you will have to do something about it. Sleeping with other people is often challenging. The heat from their body can make it difficult for you to sleep well, especially if your body is super sensitive.

Take time to sit with your partner and discuss the situation. Ensure that he or she is in a good mood before opening up. Besides, ensure that you and your partner did not have any issue recently, before bringing it up.

## Analyze Your Habituation

Habituation refers to the process of adapting to new surroundings or a set of stimuli. For example, you might find it difficult to sleep in a noisy environment, such as a typical city, with blaring honks and barking dogs. However, you will discover that those sounds will stop being an issue in the long run.

Interestingly, it becomes an issue to sleep well again when you find yourself in more serene surroundings later. The quietness will become a problem for you. You might start getting anxious when you are not hearing sounds in the night, which affects your sleep.

If you find yourself in this situation, you might need to consider music as an alternative to the sounds you are used to hearing. It's strange to discover this. Nonetheless, the reality is that some acceptable levels of "noise" are what you need for restorative sleep.

## Chapter Five

## Making Your Bedroom A Sanctuary

You might never realize how much the atmosphere of our room affects your sleep until you make some changes. Your bedroom is supposed to be that place you can be where you feel safe from the troubles of the world. It ought to be a sanctuary that offers you relaxation immediately when you enter it.

However, this is not the experience of many. For some people, their bedrooms increase their stress level because of its atmosphere. In an ideal situation, your bedroom should feel cool and dark. It is in that kind of atmosphere that you can easily fall asleep and wake up refreshed.

You will struggle to have a quality sleep when you have a street light shimmering through your window, into your room. In that case, you will have to hang up light-blocking curtains to restore the needed darkness and coolness to your bedroom. According to researchers, only about 40 percent of all people wake up feeling truly rested. This data was released by YouGov Data. (6)

This section will explore various tactics that can enable you to create a relaxing and conducive atmosphere in your room. Once you get, and apply, these strategies, you will turn your bedroom into a sanctuary where restorative sleep is the order of the day.

## Buy A Comfortable And Relaxing Bed

Your bed is the most important component of your bedroom. So, you must not take it for granted. The first thing you need to do to make your bedroom a sanctuary is to ensure that your bed offers you the support you need to have a restorative sleep.

The quality of your mattress also matters. A fantastic mattress will offer you optimum support on all the pressure points in your body. This support ensures that you don't wake up sore. So, don't be stingy to yourself. The essence of making money is to use it to improve the quality of our lives and others.

Therefore, you should not hesitate to buy a new bed that will offer you a relaxing and refreshing sleep you deserve. Ensure that you follow the manufacturer's instructions when taking care of it, to prevent it from sagging or experiencing wear, which does not bode well for your objective of making your bedroom a sanctuary.

## Ensure You Have Comfortable Bedding

Your effort to get restorative sleep will still be futile if you get a quality bed but have low-grade bedding. You need blankets that provide warmth and pillows that offer support. When these two are missing, you cannot have the relaxing sleep you desire.

So, it is not good enough to have a comfortable bed. You should also invest in quality pillows and blankets. You need them to envelope you in your bed and give you the feeling that you are in that place where you are away from the troubles of this world.

## Make Your Room More Spacious

One of the reasons some people do not feel relaxed and comfortable in their bedrooms is that they can hardly breathe in there. What I mean by this is that they have excessive items cluttering the room, making it difficult to even move around.

If your room has this description, you have to do something about it. You need to take time to declutter it. There are many techniques that can help you create space in your home by eliminating the items you don't need.

One of them is by giving away one item daily for a week. In some cases, the reason your room has too many items is that you need to relocate some of them to another place in your home. If you find out that is the case in your bedroom, move them to another room to enjoy new soothing experiences.

## Leverage Essential Oils

Many people are taking advantage of aromatherapy to relax their bodies and prepare themselves to sleep like babies. Essential oils contain the ingredients that can make you unwind, relax, and drift off to sleep. So, you should consider using them to improve the quality of your sleep.

Some of the most popular options are lavender and vanilla. They help you to find yourself in an atmosphere where you will feel mentally and physically relaxed. You can consider buying them to bring in a special effect that will make you look forward to entering your room.

To make the best of the sweet smell of essential oils, use a diffuser or vaporizer to quickly dispense the smell throughout the entire room. Fill your room with this appealing scent to give it a temple ambience that will make you fall seamlessly into a restorative sleep.

## Furniture Position

The arrangement of your furniture can affect the spaciousness of your room. In some cases, your room will feel too small because of the way you have arranged your furniture. So, you need to take a look at the arrangement again and make the necessary adjustments.

Look at the distance between the bed and the door. If the bed is too close to the door, you will find it difficult to walk freely. So, don't hesitate to change the position. Ideally, your bed should be far from the door.

## Chapter Six

## More Ways Of Restoring Rest

You don't need sophisticated activities to restore your rest. In this chapter, you will find more tips that will not require radical changes to your life to restore your rest.

**Use Snooze Responsibly**

Before setting the alarm, think twice about it. You must be sure that you will wake up once the alarm goes off. It is crucial that you are disciplined enough to sleep for the right amount of time when you set the alarm. If you are sleeping late, then change the alarm time, if your schedule permits it.

If you leave your alarm the way it is, when you know the time set is not realistic, you will only end up hitting snooze repeatedly, which does not bode well for your aim of getting restorative sleep. The alarm will go off again, before you have barely slept enough. You will have to repeat the process again.

Therefore, it is in your best interest to set your alarm to a time you can realistically wake up to. If your alarm goes off and you feel that you need more sleep, then extend the time, rather than hitting snooze. You will only end up waking up feeling tired with that approach.

## Use Earplugs

This hint is particularly important if you are living in a place where your neighbours are having wild late-night parties. You will need earplugs to reduce the volume of the noise, so that you can sleep well.

## Avoid Sleeping With Pets

Many people see sleeping with their pets as a sign of love and affection for their furry friends. A study by the American Kennel Club (AKC) shows that 45 percent of pet owners sleep with their pets. Indeed, it is a pleasurable experience for many people who do it.

However, it is counterproductive for many individuals who share the same bed with their family pet. This difficulty is due to the fact that some animals snore, toss, and turn or breathe loudly, which makes it difficult to fall asleep or stay asleep.

Besides, young puppies have a knack of waking up and doing the same to you, asking you to take them outside. Also, cats are nocturnal, and their tendency to stay awake in the early hours of the morning can affect your sleep. (7) Therefore, you should not sleep with your pet just because others are doing so. You need to be sure that the arrangement will not disturb your sleep.

## Open Your Window

It is amazing to realize how much difference opening your window can make. It ensures that fresh air comes in to replace the stuffy air to give your bedroom a fresh and conducive atmosphere for restorative sleep.

**Try A Leg Pillow**

Most people only use pillows for their heads. However, you can make yourself more comfortable by using a leg pillow. This option is a fantastic choice, especially if you have lower back discomfort. The pain does not have to be extreme to hurt you. Slight discomfort is enough to ensure that you don't have restorative sleep.

So, you can make life easier for yourself by using a leg pillow to reposition your lower spine to reduce pain. Your hips will align, and your lower back will be in a better position when you place a pillow between your legs.

## Use A Fan

You need an air circulator in your bedroom to cool things down and help you feel free and relaxed. Plug in a fan for this purpose. This tip is especially useful during the summer months when the temperature of your room will be higher.

## Avoid Nicotine Late In The Night

Just like caffeine, nicotine is a stimulant. In other words, it works to keep you active. Taking it might help during the day, but it will be counterproductive in the night. It will affect your sleep by keeping you awake for more than you want.

## Wear Socks

If you have cold feet, you will find it challenging to sleep because your body will be struggling to regulate the remaining parts of your body. So, you might need to wear socks to ensure that you keep your feet warm to get a restorative night rest.

## Invest In A White Noise Machine

If you are living in an environment with consistent traffic noise, you might find it challenging to sleep. Indeed, you might end up getting used to it in the long run. However, in the meantime, you can buy a white noise machine. Research has proven that patients in an ICU slept better when exposed to white noise. Parents also usually use this machine to put a cranky baby to sleep. (8)

## Get Starscape

If you have experienced the delight of sleeping out under the stars in a sleeping bag before, you can replicate it in your bedroom with one of the projection machines that they now sell. Different brands have unique features to satisfy customers. Choose the one you feel will be the best for you and watch the quality of your sleep improve dramatically.

## Avoid Taking Sleeping Pills

Sleeping pills are short-term solutions to sleeping problems. They might help you to sleep better initially, but it is a problem when your body depends on them to sleep.

So, it is in your best interest to make lifestyle changes that can improve your sleep, rather than depend on drugs. You have been exposed to many ways you can improve the quality of your sleep in this book, apart from medication. Leverage them rather than depend on drugs.

Besides, sleeping pills have side effects, just like other medications. So, you will be doing yourself a great favour by avoiding them.

**Enjoy The Sun More**

Exposure to sunshine, especially in the morning, has many benefits. For example, it is a good source of vitamin D. Besides, it can help you to sleep better by resetting your body's sleep/wake cycle.

**Read Yourself Into Your Dreamland**

It is a wrong notion to assume that bedtime stories are only for children. Adults can also take advantage of this relaxing practice. Note that the kind of book you read determines the level of relaxation you will get from this activity.

Therefore, it is crucial that you pick a book that is simple to read with a good flow. You can ask your loved ones to recommend good ones, if you are not sure about picking a book that will be worth your time.

Research has proven that reading a six-minute bedtime story can improve the quality of your sleep. If you don't like reading, listening to an audiobook can also have the same effect. (10)

## Be Grateful

Scientists have discovered that gratitude and a sense of well-being are often needed to gain restorative rest. Studies have also proven that if you practice daily gratitude, then you will experience positive physical effects.

The benefits include lower blood pressure, reduced anxiety, less depression, and better sleep. According to Robert A. Emmons, a professor of psychology at UC Davis, keeping a journal of gratitude is one of the best ways to have positive feelings, which bodes well for your desire to get restorative sleep and rest. (9)

# Chapter Seven

# Leveraging Yoga For Restorative Sleeps

From East to West, yoga has travelled around the world to different cultures to establish itself as a popular practice. Many people around the world are realizing the benefits of practicing yoga, and they are committing to it. It offers calmness and relaxation that makes people feel in charge of their lives again.

Practicing yoga regularly also improves sleep, among other

benefits. This chapter will explore the benefits of yoga practice and how you can leverage it to have a restorative sleep.

## The Link Between Yoga And Restorative Sleep

From anecdotal data and research, practicing yoga has the following benefits:

## Enables You To Take A Breather

You will crash if you keep running at the pace of the modern world. You need periods when you take things slowly to come up with better strategies for enhanced performance. Yoga offers the platform to do so.

## Relaxation Of The Body

Yoga brings the body into a state of tranquillity, which soothes it and makes it relaxed.

## Relaxation Of The Mind

One of the best ways you can restore inner peace is by practicing yoga. This practice ensures that you focus on the moment, and that makes you let go of anxiety and depression.

## Generation Of Positive Emotions

You need to see life beyond your current problems to be optimistic about the future. Yoga helps you to transcend your present issues, thereby restoring inner tranquillity.

## Increased Self-Awareness

Life often threatens to make you lose sight of your abilities and strengths.

However, yoga can help you take a close look at yourself and appreciate yourself again. Note that you need to value yourself to have self-confidence and self-esteem, which leads to high self-efficacy.

## Yoga Tips

Now that you understand the benefits of practicing yoga, you are set for tips that can help you practice effectively. Here they are:

## Try A Variety Of Poses

Don't quit because you tried a pose and it seems you didn't achieve a reasonable result. Try different poses and choose the ones that give you the calmness and relaxation you crave. Besides, you should try a pose for an extended period before evaluating its effectiveness.

## Use Accessories

Do all you can to get the best out of your yoga practice. Leverage pads, straps, blankets, pillows, bolsters, or blocks to support yourself for an extended period. Nothing should stop you or discourage you from achieving the sense of peace and calmness you desire.

## Choose Somewhere Quiet And Free From Distractions

You should practice somewhere you can concentrate to have the best yoga experience. Physical and mental relaxation is only possible when you are in a quiet environment.

## Practice For A Specified Period

You can start practicing yoga for ten to fifteen minutes. Increase it later if you want more. Nonetheless, ensure that you are consistent.

# Chapter Eight

# Sign In And Out In Grand Style

Sleep is an upgrade on rest. Nonetheless, you need both for sleep to be restorative. The truth is that you cannot have restorative rest without restorative sleep. They are two sides of the same coin that cannot exist independently. So, you should be working on both, rather than on one, to have the best experience.

In this last chapter, we will reiterate the benefits of restorative sleep and also some crucial sleep-related concepts you need to understand to deepen your knowledge about this topic.

## Why You Need Restorative Sleeps And Rest

When you are sleeping, your body is carrying out a lot of activities, including repairing your muscles.

It also carries out some processes and metabolisms, such as digestion and the breakdown of substances ingested. These activities are responsible for the hangover effect you have in the morning after heavy drinking the previous night. Your body will try to ensure that the substance does not affect your organs, by converting it to a beneficial form.

So, you will reduce the pressure on your bodily system by drinking moderately. Your body also repairs your cells and mental functions when you are sleeping. Therefore, having a restorative sleep enhances your learning abilities and memory. It also enhances your ability to manage stress and your emotions successfully.

Note that you will be able to make better decisions when you have control over your stress levels and your emotions. Meanwhile, when you make quality decisions, you will get better results, which bodes well for your mental and physical health.

However, you cannot enjoy these benefits if you don't enter deep and

REM sleep. This stage of sleep is when the body and mind truly come together. Experts refer to them as the 'restorative sleep' phase. Therefore, it is crucial that we explore them.

## REM Sleep

REM sleep is interesting in various ways. It stands for Rapid Eye Movement sleep. During this stage, your body is not active, but your mind is carrying out a lot of activities. These actions are the reason you have dreams, and sometimes, nightmares.

For some people, their bodies act in similar ways during REM as it does when they are awake. The body is shut down. However, it will still exhibit restricted movements.

Experts believe that this phase of sleep is needed for emotional processing of events and memory formatting. Studies have shown that REM sleep improves our ability to develop new skills and learn. (10)

## Deep Sleep

Your blood pressure and breathing rate are crucial factors that show that you have entered into a deep sleep. In a deep sleep phase, your heart rate and blood pressure will start slowing down. Brain waves in this stage are also slow and enlarged.

You need to get to this phase to enjoy restorative physical and emotional rest. When you are in a deep sleep, hormones in your body, that promote growth and healing, will be released. Besides, your immune system also gets stronger, and your body will go through a complete renewal process. (9)

When you don't sleep at night, your body will struggle to attain deep sleep the following night. The good news is that you can still catch up if you improve the quality of your sleep subsequently.

In ideal conditions, you will be in the deep sleep phase for the first third of the night, while the final part will be made up of REM sleep. Sleep experts recommend that you sleep seven to nine hours a night. However, you will not need to sleep that much to feel rejuvenated and rested as you grow older.

## How To Sign In And Out In Style

As we start to conclude this book, let's explore some crucial tips that can help you sleep peacefully and wake up rejuvenated. Here they are:

## Have A Stable Sleep Schedule

As earlier mentioned, you will not need to sleep up to seven to nine hours to feel refreshed as you grow older. Nonetheless, you have to maintain a consistent sleep schedule.

You will give your body the needed stability to carry out its activities when you have a regular time you sleep and wake up. When you sleep at a particular time every day, you will realize that you will wake up around the same period, even without an alarm.

## Watch Out For Sleep Stealers

The quality of your sleep is not only affected by the things you do before you sleep but your general activities during the waking day. For example, drinking caffeine and alcohol are potential sleep stealers.

Regular exercise can improve the quality of your sleep. However, it can steal your sleep when it is excessive. It can lead to body pain, which prevents you from enjoying a restorative sleep. So, ensure that you are not involved in activities that can take their toll on your night's rest during the day.

## Learn The Art of Relaxation

All through this book, what you have been learning is the art of relaxation. Don't allow society to put pressure on you to rush such that you forget how to rest. If you don't allow your body to rest, it will force you to do it. How? When you fall sick.

You are not a machine. Even machines have to be maintained to prevent them from breaking down. So, you need to start taking your sleep and rest seriously. You already have the information you need to change your life.


It is now time to put in practice what you have learned. There is no point in reading this book if you are not ready to utilize the information in it. So, leverage the tips you have learned and apply it to your life. You are about to have a new lease on life, by having more restorative sleep, seamlessly, as you do so.

**Thank you for reading this book!**

If you found this book helpful, I would be grateful if you would post an honest review on Amazon so this book can reach and help other people. All you need to do is to visit: amazon.com/author/senseipauldavid click the correct book cover, and finally click on the blue link next to the yellow stars that says, "customer reviews."

## To Check Out The Next Book In This Series Visit:

www.amazon.com/author/senseipauldavid

www.senseipublishing.com

@senseipublishing
#senseipublishing

Check out our recommendations for other books for adults & kids plus other great resources by visiting:

www.senseipublishing.com/resources/

## Join Our Publishing Journey!

If you would like to receive FREE BOOKS, and get to know us better, please click www.senseipublishing.com and join our newsletter by entering your email address in the pop-up box.

## Get Our FREE Books Today!

Click & Share the Links Below

### FREE Kids Books

lifeofbailey.senseipublishing.com
kidsonearth.senseipublishing.com

### FREE Self-Development Book

senseiselfdevelopment.senseipublishing.com

Restoring Restorative Rest

## Experience Over 25 FREE Engaging Guided Meditations!

Prized Skills & Practices for Adults & Kids. Help Restore Deep-Sleep, Lower Stress, Improve Posture, Navigate Uncertainty & More.

Download the Free Insight Timer App and click the link below:

**http://insig.ht/sensei_paul**

If you like these meditations & want to go deeper, email me for a FREE 30min LIVE Coaching Session:
**senseipauldavid@senseipublishing.com**

## About the Author

I create simple & transformative eBooks & Guided Meditations for Adults & Children, proven to help navigate uncertainty, solve niche problems & bring families closer together.

I'm a former finance project manager, private pilot, jiu-jitsu instructor, musician & former University of Toronto Fitness Trainer. I prefer a science-based approach to focus on these & other areas in my life, to stay humble & hungry to evolve. I hope you enjoy my work and I'd love to hear your feedback.

- It's a great day to be alive!
Sensei Paul David

Scan & Follow/Like/Subscribe:
Facebook, Instagram, YouTube:
@senseipublishing

This book is not authorized for free distribution or copying

# Index

1. Michigan Medicines C.S. Mott Children's Hospital Stress Management: Relaxing You, By: Healthwise Staff, Patrice Burgess, MD, FAAFP - Family Medicine & Kathleen Romito, MD – Family. Published: December

https://www.mottchildren.org/health-library/uz220

2. Michigan Medicines C.S. Mott Children's Hospital Stress Management: Stress Management: Doing Guided Imagery to Relax. By: Patrice Burgess, MD, FAAFP - Family Medicine & Kathleen Romito, MD - Family Medicine & Adam Husney, MD - Family Medicine & Christine R.

Maldonado, Ph.D. - Behavioral Health. Published: December 15, 2009... https://www.mottchildren.org/health-library/uz2209

3. Effect of continuous heat exposure on sleep stages in humans. By: Liberty JP, Di Nisi J, Fukuda H, Muzet A, Ehrhart J, Amoros C. Published: 1989.

https://www.mottchildren.org/health-library/uz2209

4. Effects of playing a computer game using a bright display on presleep physiological variables, sleep latency, slow-wave sleep, and REM sleep.

By: J Higuchi S, Motohashi Y, Liu Y, Maeda A.

Published: 2005.

https://pubmed.ncbi.nlm.nih.gov/16120101/

5. The impact of light from computer monitors on melatonin levels in college students. Neuro Endocrinol Letter

Published: 2011. https://www.researchgate.net/publication/51107485_The_impact_of_light_from_computer_monitors_on_melatonin_levels_in_college_students

6. YouGov America: 40% of Americans don't generally wake up feeling well-rested By: Jamie Ballard.

Published: March 13, 2019.

American Kennel Club (AKC): Where do Dogs Sleep at Night

By: Erika Mansourian.

Published: August 5, 2015.

https://www.akc.org/expert-advice/lifestyle/where-dogs-sleep-night/#:~:text=In%20fact%2C%20the%

20majority%20of,crate%20their%20dog%20at%20bedtime.

7. Effect of white noise on sleep in patients admitted to coronary care.

By: Farokhnezhad Afshar P, Bahramnejad F, Asgari P, and Shiri M J Caring Sci.

Published 2016.

https://www.ncbi.nlm.nih.gov/pmc/articles/PMC4923834/#:~:text=A%20study%20by%20Stanchina%20et,noises%20recorded%20in%20ICU%20environment

8. Why it Pays to Read

By: Rebecca Gross.

Published: January 16, 2015.

https://www.arts.gov/art-works/2015/why-it-pays-read

9. Understanding Sleep

By: Institute's Brain Resources and Information Network (BRAIN)

Published: 2019,

https://www.ninds.nih.gov/Disorders/Patient-Caregiver-Education/understanding-Sleep


10. Sleep Disorders,

By: National Cancer Institute

Published: 2020.

https://www.cancer.gov/about-cancer/treatment/side-effects/sleep-disorders-hp-pdq

www.ingramcontent.com/pod-product-compliance
Lightning Source LLC
Chambersburg PA
CBHW071716040426
42446CB00011B/2094